Other Books by Gladys Conklin

Lucky Ladybugs

by GLADYS CONKLIN

drawings by GLEN ROUNDS

Holiday House, Inc. • New York

to Giselle, the little girl who said,
"We don't kill ladybugs—they're good!"

The Mother Goose rhyme that begins

> *Ladybug, ladybug, fly away home,*
> *Your house is on fire,*
> *Your children do roam,*

is known to boys and girls all over the world. It probably started in Europe hundreds and hundreds of years ago. After the hops were harvested, the dry vines were burned. This was one way to get rid of the aphids, but it very likely burned many ladybugs that were on the vines, too.

Long ago, ladybugs were dedicated to the Virgin Mary because of their help to man. They were called "Beetles of Our Lady." Ladybugs are still honored in many countries, and each has its own pet name for them. In England they are called "Ladybirds." Swedish farmers call them "The Virgin Mary's Golden Hens," and in France they are called "The Cows of the Lord."

—GLADYS CONKLIN

A ladybug is lucky.
She does not need to fly
away home. She has a new
home every day.

Her house can't burn.
It is a blade of grass,
a leaf on a rose bush,
or in the center of a daisy.

A ladybug wouldn't know
her children if she saw them.
She lays her tiny yellow eggs on
a leaf and flies away and leaves them.

In about five days the eggs
hatch into baby ladybugs.
A baby ladybug is called a larva.
It doesn't look anything like
its parents. But it eats the
same kind of food.

These little larvae are
lizard-like creatures that run
rapidly on six long black legs.
Their long pointed bodies are often
marked with orange or blue.
The larvae have greedy appetites
and eat tiny insects called aphids.
They eat all day long and grow fast.
In about three weeks they are ready
to turn into pupas.

A pupa rests for a week.
It can't walk around but
will jerk up and down when
bothered. The sun warms it.
The wind blows on it.
Inside the pupal shell
a wonderful thing is happening.
The little larva is changing
into an adult ladybug.

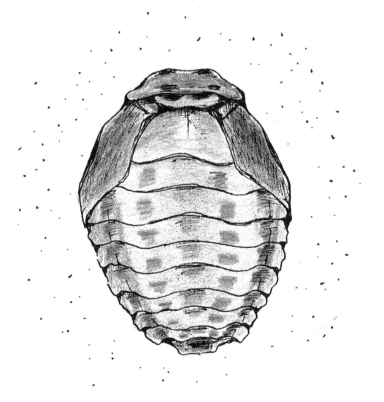

One day the pupal shell splits open.
Out crawls a pale ladybug.
It sits quietly, waiting
for its body to dry and harden.
Slowly its color deepens
and black spots appear on its back.
Now it is ready to fly.

Most ladybugs wear shiny polka-dot dresses
of red with black dots.
Some have two dots. Others have five,
seven, and even fifteen dots. Some are
plain red with no dots.

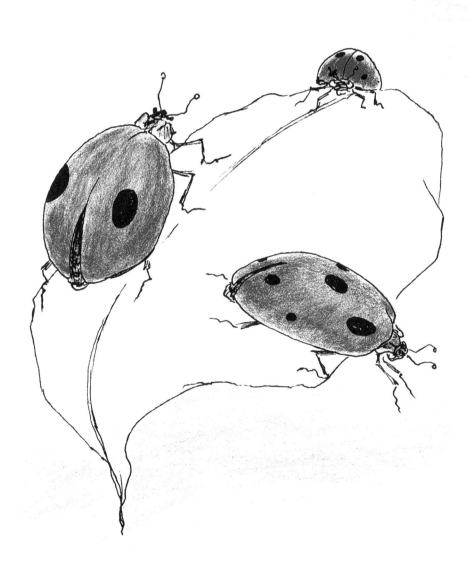

A ladybug is really a beetle,
and its real name
is ladybird beetle.

When the sun is shining,
ladybugs busily crawl
around on leaves, or rosebuds,
or blades of grass.
They are hunting for aphids.
They eat dozens of them every day.

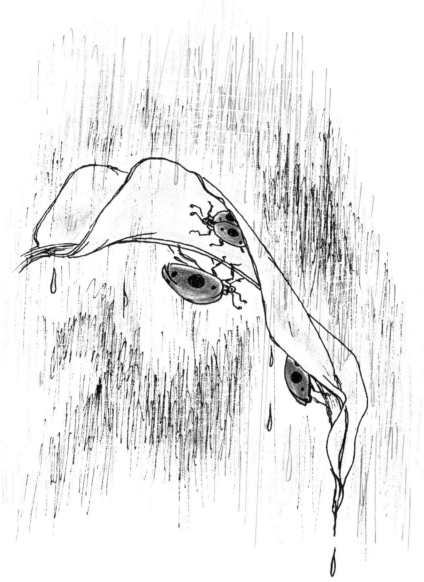

When it rains, ladybugs crawl
under a leaf and keep dry.
When the rain stops, they open
their hard wing covers, unfold
their delicate flying wings,
and depart to new places.

A ladybug keeps itself very clean.
When it finishes eating, it
washes its face with its front legs.
Then it holds each front leg up to
its mouth and carefully nibbles it
until it is completely clean.
The other legs are briskly
rubbed together to clean them.

When the days become cold,
ladybugs hunt for a warm
place to spend the winter.
Sometimes they creep into cracks
in houses or barns, or sleep snug
and warm under haystacks.

In some places, all the ladybugs
for miles around gather into a cloud—
thousands and thousands of them—
and fly to the mountains.

They crawl under rocks, or loose
bark on trees, or creep under
heaps of dry leaves.

In some of the southwestern states
tons of ladybugs are scooped into sacks.
They are kept in cold storage until
the following spring.

Then the farmers buy them by the quart
or the gallon. The ladybugs are set free in the
fields and spend their days eating aphids.

In the mountains,
there is a rush of activity as the
ladybugs come out of their deep sleep.
The tree trunks and rocks turn bright red
as the mass of thousands of ladybugs starts to move.

Soon the air is filled with a
silent swarm of tiny scarlet beetles.
They circle higher and higher,
up and up until they meet
the prevailing winds.
Then they ride the airways back to the fields
and gardens in the valleys below.

Ladybugs are lucky!
Birds do not like the taste of them.
People like to have them in their gardens.
There is always plenty of food for them to eat.
Ladybugs are found all over the world.
They are welcomed in every country.

Many people consider it a sign of
good luck when a ladybug lands on them.
There is a story that long ago some
grain fields were being destroyed by aphids.
In answer to prayers, a swarm of little
red beetles appeared and ate the aphids.
Since that time, ladybugs have been
known as a special friend of man.

When you find a ladybug,
hold it gently on your finger
and let it fly away.
It may be lucky for you.

GLADYS CONKLIN is an active naturalist herself and writes from first-hand knowledge of children's curiosity about small wild creatures. Until her recent retirement, she was head of the Children's Department of the Hayward, California, Public Library, and, in response to the children's interest in natural science, helped them found the Hayward Library Bug Club. Its members have inspired her to write six previous books, I LIKE CATERPILLARS, I LIKE BUTTERFLIES, WE LIKE BUGS, IF I WERE A BIRD, THE BUG CLUB BOOK, and I CAUGHT A LIZARD.

Mrs. Conklin and her husband, formerly of the U.S. Lighthouse Service, live in San Lorenzo, California and spend vacations on camping trips in the United States and Mexico.

GLEN ROUNDS has illustrated dozens of books about the outdoor world, most of them works that he has also written from his own observations of wild creatures.

OL' PAUL, THE MIGHTY LOGGER, published more than thirty years ago, began his career as author and artist, and his long list of titles since then includes THE BLIND COLT, WILD ORPHAN, BILLY BOY, THE TREELESS PLAINS, and other books about nature, animals, folklore, life in the West and pioneering.

Mr. Rounds was born in the South Dakota Badlands, grew up on a Montana ranch, and later roamed the country as logger, sign painter, muleskinner, baker, sideshow medicine man, and cowpuncher. He now lives in Southern Pines, North Carolina.